Lescene Productions

Deeper Insights

A Collection Of Expressed Feelings And Nurtured Articulations Of A Young Male's Feelings

By

Ellis Witter

Deeper Insights

ISBN: 978-1-7392124-1-4

LESCENE PRODUCTIONS

LESCENE PRODUCTIONS PRESENTS

DEEPER INSIGHTS

A COLLECTION OF EXPRESSED FEELINGS AND NURTURED ARTICULATIONS OF A YOUNG MALE'S FEELINGS

BY ELLIS WITTER

Eboni #FutureBoss

I'm very proud of the person you have become, seeing you grow and elevate is inspiring.

Thank you for all of the love and support

Keep being you regardless the world needs more people like you

EW

Table of Contents

Overview

Men's emotions are often met with a deep fear of judgment, lack of support (Both publicly and privately), and fear of belittlement. I hope this book is able to shift these mindsets and allow you to re-think men's emotions, especially young men who often fall victim to toxic traits passed down from hurtful comments, older generations with closed-minded & repetitive thought cycles, and the burden of bottling up emotions and leaving trauma undealt with. We all have feelings, and these are mine, expressed with pure honesty. I know you may relate.

I dedicate this to everyone who is afraid of speaking about their emotions. No matter who you are or where you are in your journey.

I also dedicate this to those suffering in silence.

A Word From The Author

These are all poems of my heart's expressions. This is cringe and embarrassing (for me, at least)

but there is an importance in reflecting and learning from experiences and situations as you grow through life. I made sure to express my emotions healthily and honestly.

"Releasing a Poetry book is a huge achievement, but it isn't the scariest part for me. It's the collective of poems I've written mainly about my feelings. Most of which I'm afraid even to show the person it's about."

"It's an incredible insight into me, and I hope that I can not only Inspire those facing similar situations but to continue doing things I never believed I could do."

"Being publicly vulnerable is daunting but needed, and I am here to show you the world it's nothing to be afraid of or shamed for."

I hope you enjoy it!

My Dyslexia is not a word or an excuse to hold me back from things I do.

It is not a form of weakness.

It's a strength!

It motivates me to show myself that anything's possible and not to underestimate myself.

That Age

Ok, so I'm at that age,

Or place of my mind.

Whereas much I don't really want to,

Or mean any disrespect by it.

I can't help but notice

How much I appreciate a woman's natural beauty,

And there… Physic.

If you get what I mean,

And I don't mean to

That Age

Nor mean any ill intentions by it,

But I mean, c'mon

I'm at the age, I'm new to this world, and there are many beautiful women on this earth.

So although I am so focused on my grind etc.,

I can't help but think to myself.

I wonder what it would be like to be her boyfriend, etc.

Now, the real question is,

Am I thinking with my head or with my dick?

Sometimes, the thought patterns get mixed up,

And I can't really help it,

I'm a young male with a lot of testosterone,

And I need to channel it correctly.

I know I have to; I can't be reckless with it.

So now I have to learn discipline,

Which I'm doing well at,

But when the next time comes…

I owe it to myself to navigate it effectively

And efficiently.

It isn't easy.

Emotions are beautiful and
unique.

Sometimes they can get confusing.

Do not recriminate or
suppress them.

They are you,

Embrace them.

Express them.

A Matter Of My Heart

So here I am again, back in the same place I was before

Older but still war-torn.

Over my arch-nemesis, Infatuation.

A form of lust or a desire for love?

Something which my mind neglects,

But my heart longs for.

Unfortunately, my past hasn't been kind to me.

My mind doesn't dwell on that,

As I'm conflicted between someone who likes me

And someone else I like.

I hate it,

Really and truly, I hate it.

I went for years being OK that I was alone in this journey.

I accepted and found peace in it.

Peace in solitude.

Peace in evolving, growing, and glowing.

It wasn't until recently that I noticed how brightly my light was showing.

It attracted someone to that I never knew viewed me that way.

Panicking and somewhat pressured, I danced how humans danced

And then watched her fly off,

A Matter Of My Heart

I was and still am OK.

I just can't help the feeling that I was used to.

We both got what we wanted,

But my selflessness was woven into her selfishness.

But is that fair to say?

Well, I didn't think it was until feelings were made clear.

That not even a year away, would stop her from wanting me.

Well, shit, then...

I told her that long-distance isn't for me.

We agreed but the way she has been moving,

She's reserving herself a front-row seat to my love.

Admirable but terrifying.

A Matter Of My Heart

This other girl honestly has no business being on my mind this much.

Yet, here she is,

I feel myself simping over her,

And if you were in my shoes, I doubt you'd do differently.

I'm grateful for her and her advice etc.,

But I can't stop thinking about her.

She has a man, I'm not him, but I wish I was.

To call someone like her, my girlfriend, would be a blessing.

Both of these women are blessings,

But I don't know what to do.

See, one supports me and publicly backs me,

Yet, Both of them watch me on a regular.

A Matter Of My Heart

They both like the stuff I am doing.

Yet, circumstances make me question their intentions;

One already got what she wanted from me.

And has made it clear she wants more,

Yet longevity-wise, It doesn't match up.

She does stuff (substances) that I disagree with .

Nor can justify

Yet, the other feels to me like an angel sent down to earth.

Yet, circumstances keep us apart as well.

And I don't know her true intentions.

Does she like me? Or just wants to... Imagine that one for yourselves.

A Matter Of My Heart

We hardly talk as well; it's always me popping up.

I feel like I constantly bother her, yet I love talking to her.

She did, in fact, give me her number after all,

But what good is that if you are in a relationship?

A long-term one that is

The minds of women are something I will never understand.

Regardless of what happens next, I'm still going to do me.

Continue on my grind, continue chasing my dreams

Because that's what makes me who I am

And I guess

That's also what makes them want me.

Infatuation is my biggest enemy.

A Matter Of My Heart

My lustful desires vs. my mind's purpose

Who wins in the end?

I guess we will have to wait and see.

It's ok

If you feel like you need help,

Go seek it

Your mental health is just as
important as your physical health

Do what you need to preserve it.

Victims To Our Thoughts

Yep, you read that right,

I'm a victim.

We are all victims

Victims to our thoughts,

Thoughts that toy with us,

Thoughts that tell us we should be a certain way

Or look like that person.

When are you going to get this?

You said you would do that, why haven't you?

Victims To Our Thoughts

You look fat,

You don't have what this person has, so why not.

This person has achieved A, B & C, what have you done?

You can do better than this.

IT'S ANNOYING

So fucking annoying.

The self-doubt, the constant battle within your mind.

The slight envy that builds when you compare yourself to others.

We are all guilty of it,

And we are all victims of it.

No matter what anyone gives off,

We've all fought or been fighting these battles
But the question is, who wins in the end?

It's ok to cry

Never let anybody convince you otherwise

You're Not Mine, But I Wish You Were

You're not mine, but I wish you were,

And I hate myself for not being able to express that.

I don't know what you do to me, and I hate that you are able to.

Knowing that you play on my mind constantly and I probably never on yours.

I don't like how you dance so elegantly around my brain,

And I just can't help but watch and appreciate the beauty of it.

Knowing that unless I do something drastic, you'll continue to

My heart is your playground, and you don't even know it.

You're Not Mine, But I Wish You Were

I guess I have to make peace with it. After all, this is kinda my fault,

For not being able to express this to you personally
but detail this on a doc

I don't know if this, or you, is something I'll get over.

This plague haunts me, yet it is my doing that allows it

Infatuated or appreciative?

I know which it is, yet I can't help if I can decide it.

I wish you were, but you're not mine.

Be honest with yourself

Do you like the person you see in the mirror?

Don't Feel Sorry For Me

Don't feel sorry for me,

Because what is that going to do for me?

What is it going to do for you?

Really and truly, what's the point?

No one achieves nothing.

We all self-pity more

We can connect or maybe understand someone's struggle and pain,

But what will feeling sorry do?

Don't Feel Sorry For Me

Wishing it never happened is pointless because.. whatever happened, happened.

I have a saying I like

It doesn't matter what happened to you. What matters is how you deal with it.

So my question to you,

Are you dealing with "it"? If so, how?

Obstacles will always form.

Don't let it defeat you.

Easier said than done,

Once it's done, it can always be said though.

Think differently about it.

I Don't Want To Do This Anymore

I sit next to you - I'm too shocked to say anything.

I sit far away - I wish I had said what I felt.

Guess this all comes down to my self-confidence.

Like I've stated before, I hate that you do this to me.

I don't know if I'm developing feelings for you or not ,

Because even though it's been so short.

We've really gotten to know each other really well.

I just know that it's not going to work out the way I
imagine it

I Don't Want To Do This Anymore

Never has and probably never will

So why do I keep doing this to myself?

I really don't know, yet here I am,

Ending up in situations like these.

Why do I always develop good things with girls?

Just to get played again,

I go from being confident to hating myself in 5 seconds.

It hurts even more because I love myself, and I'm healed.

Yet, I'm confessing,

Like I've been doing over the last year,

I really wish this was a dream

But there's no waking up from this.

I Don't Want To Do This Anymore

Your sleeping peacefully,

I'm red-eyed, sleep-deprived, and in my feelings.

What did it for me was when you came to my hotel room to hug and comfort me when I cried,

And even in an extremely vulnerable moment, you were there supporting & loving me.

I don't even remember the last time I cried,

Yet, you were there when I did.

Now, I'm at war with myself again,

Over a girl, again,

And I'm losing again.

No, I'm not happy about it.

Feeling incapable of feeling loved,

I Don’t Want To Do This Anymore

Is one of the worst pains,

Because I’m not even numb to it.

I’m feeling absolutely everything,

And I can’t do anything about it.

We can mock each other all day.

We all know in the end,

That we are suffering similar pains.

I'm just vocalizing mine.

That Weird Stage

I m in that weird stage in life

That weird stage between what comes next and what you leave behind.

That weird stage where you're figuring out what works for you.

What hairstyle suits me?

Do I grow out my facial hair? Should I change my style?
Am I strong enough?

Am I entirely happy with my body?

Is being here the right place for me?

Am I happy with the way everything's going?

That Weird Stage

It really is an awkward stage,

Guess I have to embrace it.

Learn how to treat Men's emotions.

We pretend that we are ok when we are not.

We are deceivingly good,

But deceivement only lasts for so long.

So Let Me Get This Straight

Us, as in men, have to

Identify someone we like.

Get to know them,

Build up confidence,

Flirt and make our intentions clear.

Ask them out,

Hope they don't reject us.

If they do, we are embarrassed & heartbroken.

So Let Me Get This Straight

If they don't, either hook up or get into a relationship.

During the course, figure out if we are compatible and if
the relationship can last.

If it does, great,

But a lot of the times, it doesn't.

I don't like it.

I don't like it at all.

Why is it always men who have to do all of this?

And the women get to decide if we are worthy or not?

I don't get it.

Nor will I conform to it,

I like the peace, so I'll stay by myself.

Besides, If women are the prize, what does that make us men?

These emotions of ours.

They can be difficult to navigate,

The constant back and forths,

But we do know what we ideally want in the end, right?

Am I Still Not Over Her/DSLM?

It's silly, really?

All this girl did was be nice to me.

Go out of her way to answer my messages.

Encourage me when I felt lost.

Gave me her number to talk more freely and direct,

And still, through all of that.

I constantly felt like a burden.

The worst part is that she doesn't know how much that meant to me.

Am I Still Not Over Her/DSLM?

I fell hard for someone who was never mine.

I wrote beautiful poetry about her,

But I could never admit that to her .

Never,

So here I am.

Somewhat suffering by myself again;

Nothing New.

A core subject of life is learning.

It never stops,

No matter how painful or stressful they appear,

There's always something new to learn.

Strange Shiftings

These past few weeks have been strange

So, much good has happened.

I've reaped the rewards of my labour.

I relax in a constant state of gratitude,

But it's been strange.

I feel like there is something wrong internally,

And I can't seem to place my finger on it.

I am arguably at one of the best and happiest points in my life.

Yet I feel… Strange,

Strange Shiftings

Something is bothering me.

Is it loneliness?

Is it lustful desires?

Does my ego need a re-look?

Or have I lost my passion?

It feels like it's none of them and all of them at the same time

I need to sit with this and figure it out

I'll come back with an update when the time feels right.

Until then, avu vour

To those who feel alone,

I wish it was a foreign feeling.

Question

What's the difference between thoughts and dreams?

Dreams Of Pain

I had a dream about you last night.

I felt in my heart, it wasn't right.

I know you don't owe me a thing,

But in my dreams, someone else gave you a ring

"Congratulations!" I said, hiding back the tears.

Knowing after years of silently suffering, I had to face

the reality of my fears.

It should have been me,

It should have been me,

Dreams Of Pain

But I know now that it'll never be me.

I smiled as I watched the guy come near

He looked like a B-tech clone of me; that much was clear,

He makes you smile.

He makes you laugh.

He makes you the happiest you've been.

I could have made you so much more if you were under my wing.

Not just under my wing but by my side.

Now, my soul is due for more lonely nights.

It's not fair, but when is life?

I've been stabbed in the back by the making of my own knife.

What a shame!

Dreams Of Pain

In so much pain,

But the feeling is neutral.

A natural girl of your beauty is by now something I'm
used to.

I watched you gimmer bright, Knowing it wasn't half-hearted.

I feel like every creature left behind when Noah's Ark
had departed.

In a world of copying others and seeking

validation,

Strive to be authentic.

In All Honesty

In all honesty,

I'll admit I'm scared.

Really scared

Scared that my projects will be on pause for another year,

Scared that I won't get any action for another year,

Scared that today, it's been a month since I last rejected the one girl who had feelings for me.

I'm scared of releasing this online and what the after effects (good & bad) might look like.

I'm scared that side of life will pass me by, and I'll have no one to blame but myself for it.

In All Honesty

I know I'll be ok,

I do certainly hope that these are not the case.

Hopefully, another product of my overthinking,

But this is where I'm at right now.

We'll see what happens next.

You are you,

And you are unique

Never forget that.

To Me, From Me

Hey Me!

First of all, I want to say I'm proud of you,

Really and truly,

I'm proud.

The progress you've made has been amazing.

Nothing less than astounding,

And I know you deep down want the world to know and appreciate it & you.

And they will,

But for now, I need you to know.

To Me, From Me

That young child inside of you. It's very proud,

It's amazing to see how you've developed and grown.

You have become that person you've always wanted to be,

And more. Much, much more.

You've done things they thought you couldn't do,

Even things you didn't believe you could do,

But you did them.

And you want what?

You smashed them!

You've made this a habit. It's almost regular to you.

You've conquered your emotions,

And they will love you for that. They will trust me

To Me, From Me

Trust yourself!

I'm very excited to see what's next in your course

What projects you'll smash and what people you'll meet/work with.

God bless you,

And may he continue to

Stay blessed, King!

And stay being you, no matter what they say or do.

With Love

Me ❤

Once we all start

Having more open and honest
conversations with each other,

We will soon realize that the things
we feel alone in

Or experiences we've gone
through, We are not the only ones.

Then, we will have better ideas of
how to best deal with them.

Self Inflicted Suffering

I hold my hands up; this is all my doing.

An unfortunate by product of the success I'm pursuing.

Growth isn't easy; neither is suffering silent pain,

But if the weather is a game, with the sun comes after some rain.

I complain about the rejection,

Yet I'm the one rejecting.

I've met shattered frames looking at me for perfection.

I'm not, nor will I be, the one to repair you.

You make up lies with me when reality provides honest confessing.

Self Inflicted Suffering

You may not like the image it paints, but we both know it's true.

I'm not getting involved with mentally unstable girls,

Nor will I wife a girl solely based on her looks and curls,

But it's not even about looks. It's about your mentality.

We can be on the same page but in two different paragraphs entirely.

I know what's right and what's good for me.

I don't deserve half-hearted love; I'd rather be free.

So, if I must play the bad guy and break your heart, I'm sorry.

Self-inflicted suffering, and I'm not allowing you anywhere near me.

Your intentions may be genuine, but I don't believe them.

Self Inflicted Suffering

You will have some hurdles to jump for me to know if
the puzzle fits.

I have to be choosy; it's just the way I am. Love me for me, accept it as well if you can.

So, before you sell yourself that idea, keep your receipt handy,

Because we all have habits of falling in love with what can be.

The truth is, I'm scared of relationships.

In relation to these seas, I'm aware of sailing.

Ships, I'm dodging the dangers and heading for peace,

But together is a path I'm afraid of intertwining.

Cause I'd prefer you whining, which one I'm still deciding.

I just need a hug and a love letter from the heart.

I feel I'm reaching my limit, undecided between a restart or a pass.

Self Inflicted Suffering

I've breezed past the limits so much that I didn't even know there was one.

Self-inflicted suffering because the pain's never fully gone.

One girl Lol'd me, yet still follows me.

I had unruly dreams of her, none of which she'll get to see.

Another hid the truth. When I found out, I dipped.

I have a habit of doing so to protect my inner peace.

All of these poems are thoughts and feelings I've said with MY chest.

Self-inflicted suffering because I know I'm different from the rest.

Truth is, there's more I could share with you.

More things that little to nobody has a clue about.

To be honest, I really could go into more detail.

Self Inflicted Suffering

These are just letters from my heart I've expressed to certain females.

Laugh at me and make your memes if it brings you thrill,

But at your lowest times, may you turn to this book for a free meal.

Even if I pay my dues for telling you all the truth,

I sit happy, alone but all together, feeling similar emotions in our rooms.

A Special Thank You

A lot of people have been here at crucial stages of my life.

You know who you are,

And you all know how much you mean to me.

I thank you from the bottom of my heart.

A special thank you to my Therapist.

If it wasn't for you, I wouldn't have had the confidence and inspiration to do this.

You've seen me at my darkest and brightest;

Thank you for being here through it all

There are way too many people to thank personally.

Just know I love and appreciate you all

E x.

About Me

I am a Black British Multi-talented Award Winning Actor, Script Writer, Model, Producer & Presenter, and Co-founder of my production company Lescene Productions.

This Poetry book serves as an honest truth of self-expression, turning my poetry into something far greater. I pray that a story or two can resonate with you and can allow me to share more.

This is only the beginning.

Contact

My Instagram is @kingellisw
My Twitter is @Elliswitter

Printed in Great Britain
by Amazon

11344347R00037

Emotional Maturity Meets Brutal Honesty

Is This Book A Prose? Poetry?,

Spoken Word? Or Something Else?

Whatever It Is,

It's More Than It Appears To Be.

It's Deceptive

It's Duplicitous

It's Deeper Insights.

ISBN 9781739212414

90000

9 781739 212414